D1799151

Trend Lines and Fibonacci Charts

(How to Read and Manage Potential Profit)

Rich Finegan

Disclaimer:

Foreign exchange trading carries a high level of risk and may not be suitable for you, please carefully consider your risk appetite and do not invest money that you cannot afford to lose

Copyright © 2015 Rich Finegan

All rights reserved.

ISBN: 1511500573
ISBN-13: 9781511500579

DEDICATION:

To those who are serious in forex trading

CONTENTS

Preface

This book is the third book on foreign exchange (forex) after the first book "Forex Trend Line Trading Strategy: It is hard to win without knowing the trend" and the second book "Forex Secret Trading Model: Tools, Timing, and Forecasting". It is recommended for reader to read those 2 books first before this going through this book so we can start with the same concept.

There is strong relationship between trend line generated from non standard Parabolic SAR (PSAR) and Fibonacci chart. If you do not know how to pick the correct starting point to draw Fibonacci chart as pointed in by non standard PSAR, it will present an incorrect Fibonacci chart.

This book will present Fibonacci Fan, Fibonacci Extension, Fibonacci Retracements charts as common tools in technical analysis to see the major and minor resistance or support of price movement. This book is expected to erase some confusion about when and how to use Fibonacci charts and also which Fibonacci chart should be set up first for analysis.

Good luck!

CHAPTER 1

TREND LINES AND FIBONACCI CHARTS

Trend lines

We have discuss about trend lines and how to draw it correctly by using non standard Parabolic SAR (PSAR) 0.02;0 in the first and second book, now we are going to combine the correct trend lines with the famous Fibonacci charts.

We are still using time frame 1 hour to set up all charts (you can modify it to any time frame)

Chart 1: Trend lines from non standard PSAR (0.02;0)

Fibonacci Charts

We are not talking about Fibonacci history and his magic number as it can be explore more by goggling it. We are going to explore the application of Fibonacci in forex trading (also applicable to other financial market trading) so we know how and when to use Fibonacci chart.

To draw a correct Fibonacci Charts, we still use non standard parabolic SAR (0.02;0) to find the starting and ending point. There are 3 kinds of Fibonacci charts that are widely used by analyst and we will explain further in next chapter on how and when to use them. We are using **high/low** (price) Fibonacci to set up these 3 Fibonacci charts.

A. Fibonacci Fan chart

Fibonacci Fan chart provides resistance and support lines (major trend lines) and also minor trend lines for future price movement.

To draw Fibonacci Fan chart, we still use the same highest and lowest price within the non standard PSAR (0.02;0). Once we draw them from technical analysis software, we will get 4 lines: the first is the original trend lines (red lines) or Major trend lines which is the same as previous trend line (resistance or support) and the other 3 lines (blue lines) are minor trend lines (see chart 2)

Chart 2: Fibonacci Fan

We are using the **latest** highest and lowest PSAR to draw Fibonacci Fan both for resistance and support. Draw the Fibonacci Fan by connecting the highest price within non standard PSAR (0.02;0) from point A to B for resistance and the lowest price within non standard PSAR (0.02;0) from point C to D for support. So it is similar to draw a trend line but you get additional 3 minor trend lines from Fibonacci Fan application. The position of those 3 minor trend lines are following the trend line slope.

B. Fibonacci Extensions chart

Fibonacci Extensions chart provides resistance and support lines (major trend lines) and also minor trend lines for future price movement.

Same as Fibonacci Fan, to draw Fibonacci Extensions chart, we still use the same highest and lowest price within the non standard PSAR groups. Once we draw the Fibonacci Extension chart (see chart 3), we will get another 6 extension lines (blue color) besides the original trend lines (red lines) or Major trend lines.

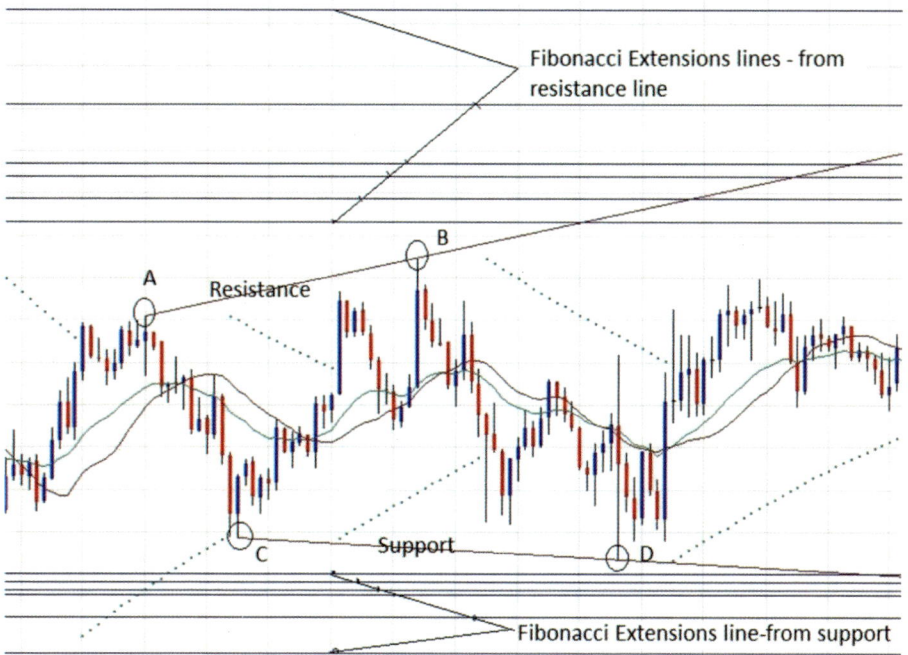

Chart 3: Fibonacci Extensions

To draw the Fibonacci Extensions chart, connect point A and B which are the highest price within the PSAR (0.02;0) to get the Resistance line (Major Trend Line) and the technical analysis software will automatically generates the extension lines from resistance. Connect point C and D which are the lowest price within the PSAR (0.02;0) to get the Support line (Major Trend Line) and the technical analysis software will automatically generates the extensions lines from support. The extensions lines are generated by using ratio: 61.8%, 100%, 138.2%, 161.8%, 261.8% and 423.6%, these are provided automatically in standard Fibonacci Extensions chart.

The position of those extensions lines are following the trend lines slope.

C. Fibonacci Retracements chart

To draw Fibonacci retracements chart, we use the **latest** highest and lowest price or the **latest** lowest and highest price within the non standard PSAR (0.02;0) group   and connect them by using technical analysis software. In Fibonacci retracements chart we will get 3 retracements lines that will act as minor support or resistance. These 3 retracements lines are using standard fibonacci ratio 38.2%, 50% and 61.8%.

In chart 4, you will get 3 retracements lines automatically from software by connecting point A (latest highest) and B (latest lowest).

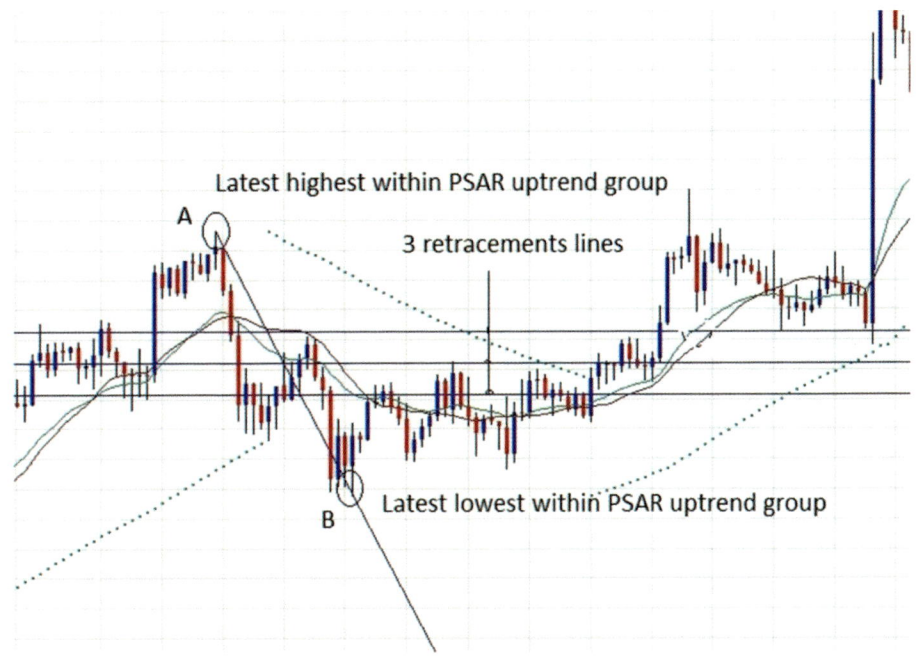

Chart 4: Fibonacci Retracements

Or you can have a starting point from the latest lowest price (point A) and connect it to the latest highest price (point B) as presented in chart 5.

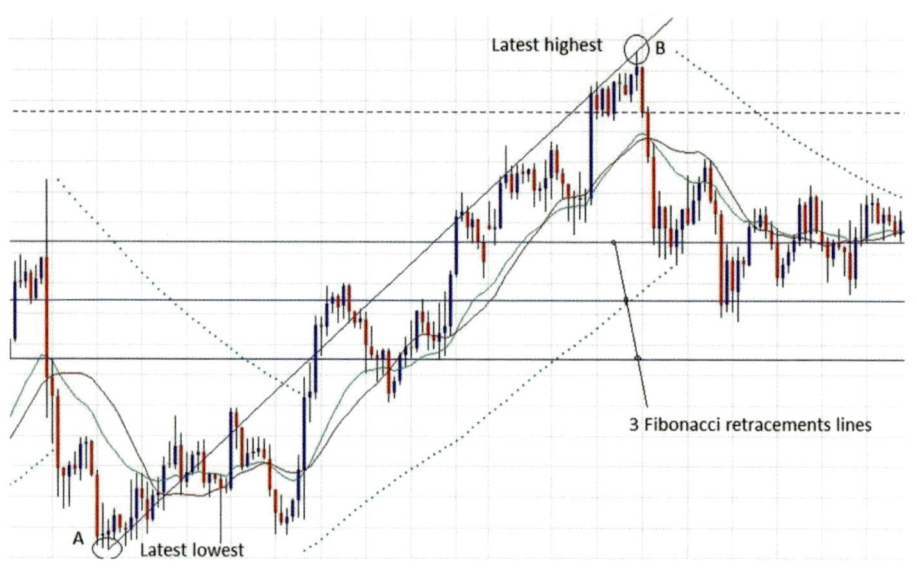

Chart 5: Fibonacci Retracements

CHAPTER 2

HOW TO READ FIBONACCI FAN CHART

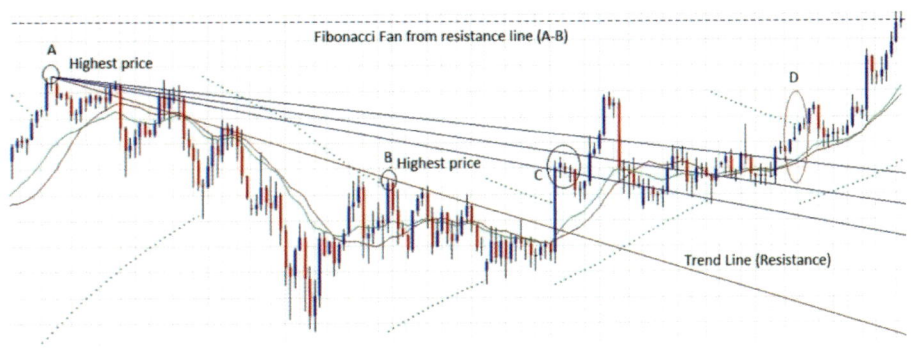

Chart 6: Fibonacci Fan

To draw Fibonacci Fan (chart 5), connect point A and B by using Fibonacci Fan application in technical analysis software to get the trend line or resistance line, the system will automatically present 3 minor trend lines (blue color).

Point C is where the price closes 2 times in a row above trend line (breaks resistance line or red color line), after that, there will be price consolidation inside the 3 minor fib. Fan trend lines. Once the **EMA 20** (green line) cross the last minor trend line (point D), there is strong chance of continuation in price.

The purpose of price movement after point C (break out) is to bring line EMA 20 to cross all the minor resistance lines, however be careful with the potential reversal after point D especially when EMA 20 cross SMA 20, price below EMA 20 and RSI <50 (see book: Forex Secret Trading model; Tools, Timing, and Forecasting for EMA 20, SMA20 and RSI 14 concept).

You may have different position of minor resistance and support lines as they depend on the slope of resistance and support line. In chart 7, they have solid minor support lines and the price can break the support and minor support line at one strike (circle A). The price is still consolidating at circle A to wait EMA 20 breaks both support and minor support lines before it continues its down trend.

Chart 7: Fibonacci Fan

CHAPTER 3

HOW TO READ FIBONACCI EXTENSIONS CHART

To draw Fibonacci Extensions (chart 8), connect point A and B to get resistance line and then point C with point D to get support line (red color), The technical analysis software will generate the extensions lines automatically both from resistance and support. Point A, B, C, D is the current available lowest and highest from non standard Parabolic SAR (0.02;0) uptrend group and down trend group in the chart.

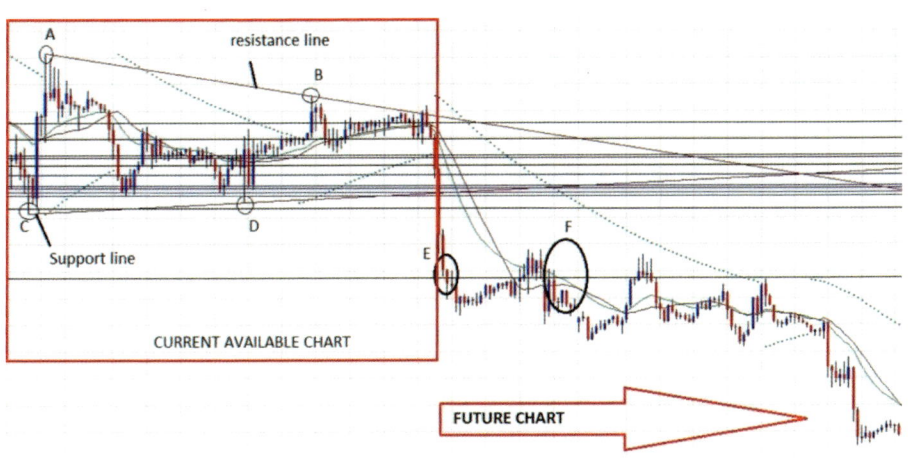

Chart 8: Fibonacci Extension

Point E is the future chart for our analysis. It is the point when the price two times close below the support line (C-D) and point F is where EMA 20 breaks all fibonacci extensions lines that generated from resistance and support lines. You can see continuation of down trend when EMA 20 breaks all those Fib. Extensions lines after point F. Now let's see another chart below:

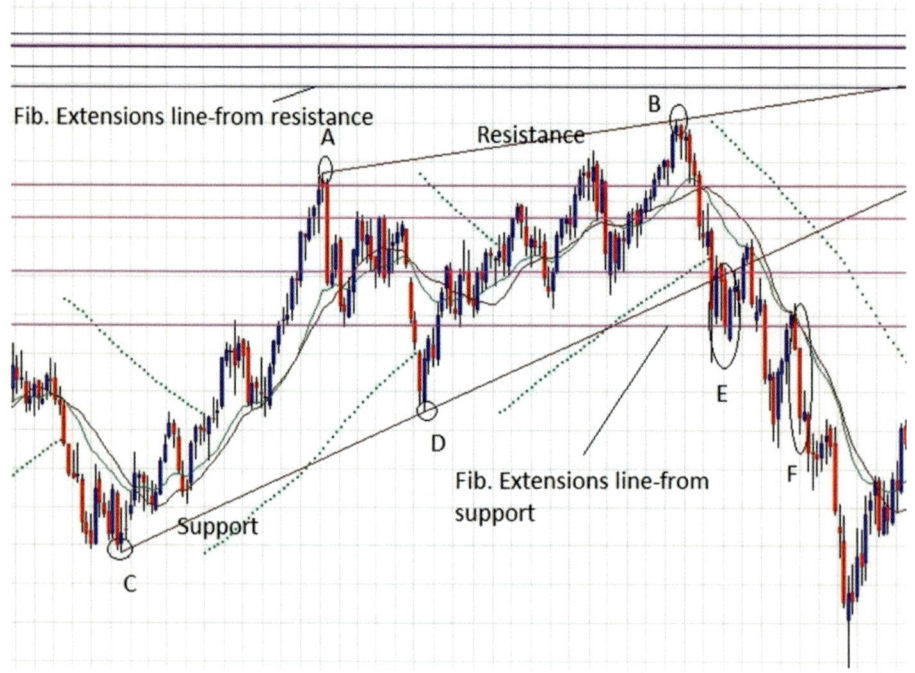

Chart 9: Fibonacci Extension

Chart 9 is another example of Fibonacci Extensions chart. Connect point A and B, it will form resistance line and Fibonacci Extensions lines from resistance (blue lines). Connect point C and D, it will form support line and Fibonacci Extensions lines from Support (pink lines).Point E is the area where price breaks support and point F is the area where EMA 20 breaks the last/lowest Fibonacci Extensions line from support (pink lines).

The down trend continuation starts at point F.

CHAPTER 4

HOW TO READ FIBONACCI RETRACEMENTS

To draw Fibonacci retracements chart, we use the latest highest and lowest price or the latest lowest and highest price within the non standard PSAR (0.02;0) and connect them by using technical analysis software. In chart 10, point A is the latest lowest and point B is the latest highest in non standard PSAR (0.02;0) group.

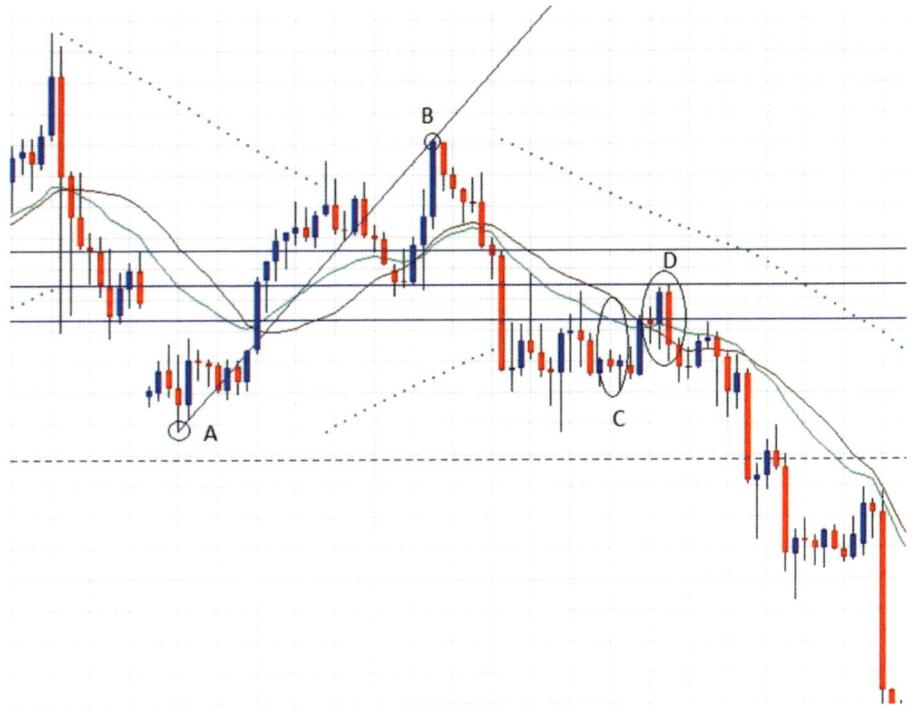

Chart 10: Fibonacci Retracements

Once we prepared the Fibonacci Retracements, EMA 20 cross the lowest line of retracements lines at point C to continue its down trend, however there is an effort to reverse the trend in point D but EMA 20 still cannot cross the lowest line of Fibonacci Retracements and the down trend keep continuing after point D.

As a rule of thumb, 3 Fibonacci Retracements lines are always between support and resistance lines and the objective of price movement is to pass EMA 20 through Fibonacci Retracements lines before any trend continuation.

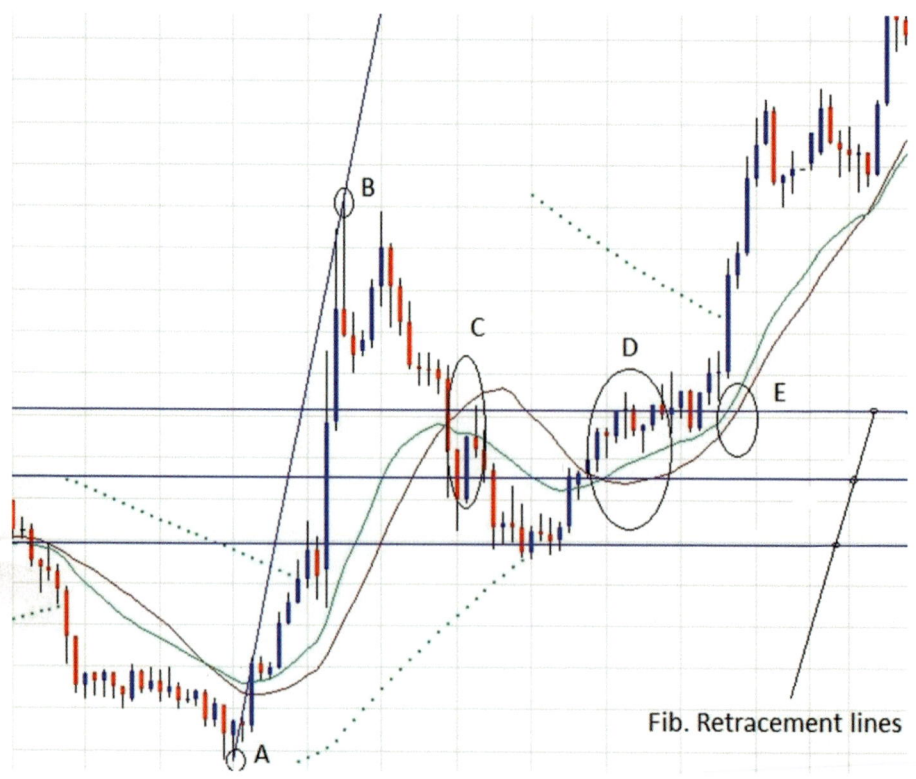

Chart 11: Fibonacci Retracements

Now let's look at chart 11, connect point A and B by using Fibonacci Retracements application and we will get 3 lines of Fibonacci retracements lines. Although the price has moved above all Fibonacci retracements lines (near point B), but EMA 20 are not breaking the top line at point C. At point C there is a reversal to avoid EMA 20 cross the top line of Fibonacci retracement and it is indicated by the price below EMA 20 (and RSI 14<50-hidden). The objective of reversal at point C is to push EMA 20 cross the lowest line of Fibonacci retracements however it has some difficulties, the price stuck and consolidates at the bottom line of Fib. Retracements and reverse again for its uptrend at point D (price above EMA 20) and the bull win when EMA 20 cross the top line at point E.

We can say that: when EMA 20 lines is still inside the Fibonacci Retracements lines, there is a chance for price volatility between bull and bear market. The bull wants EMA 20 cross the top line of Fib. Retracements line and the bear wants EMA cross the bottom line of Fib. Retracements line.

CHAPTER 5

WHICH FIBONACCI CHART
SHOULD BE USED FIRST?

In previous chapters we have discuss Fibonacci Fan, Extensions, Retracements, however there is some confusion on which Fibonacci chart need to be set up and used first. Should we use all Fibonacci charts in technical analysis in one screen?

The Fibonacci chart set up starts from:

1. Trend Line (this is part of Fibonacci chart)

2. Fibonacci Retracements chart

3. Fibonacci Fan chart

4. Fibonacci Extensions chart

1. Trend Line (Support and Resistance lines)

In chart 12, we can draw trend lines by using non standard PSAR (0.02;0). The reasons for drawing trend lines in the first step are:

- Current price is between trend lines and we can locate the price on the spot. By using EMA 20, SMA 20 and RSI 14 we can identify the price movement trend

- Trend Lines are also used for Fibonacci Fan and Extensions so we can draw it first.

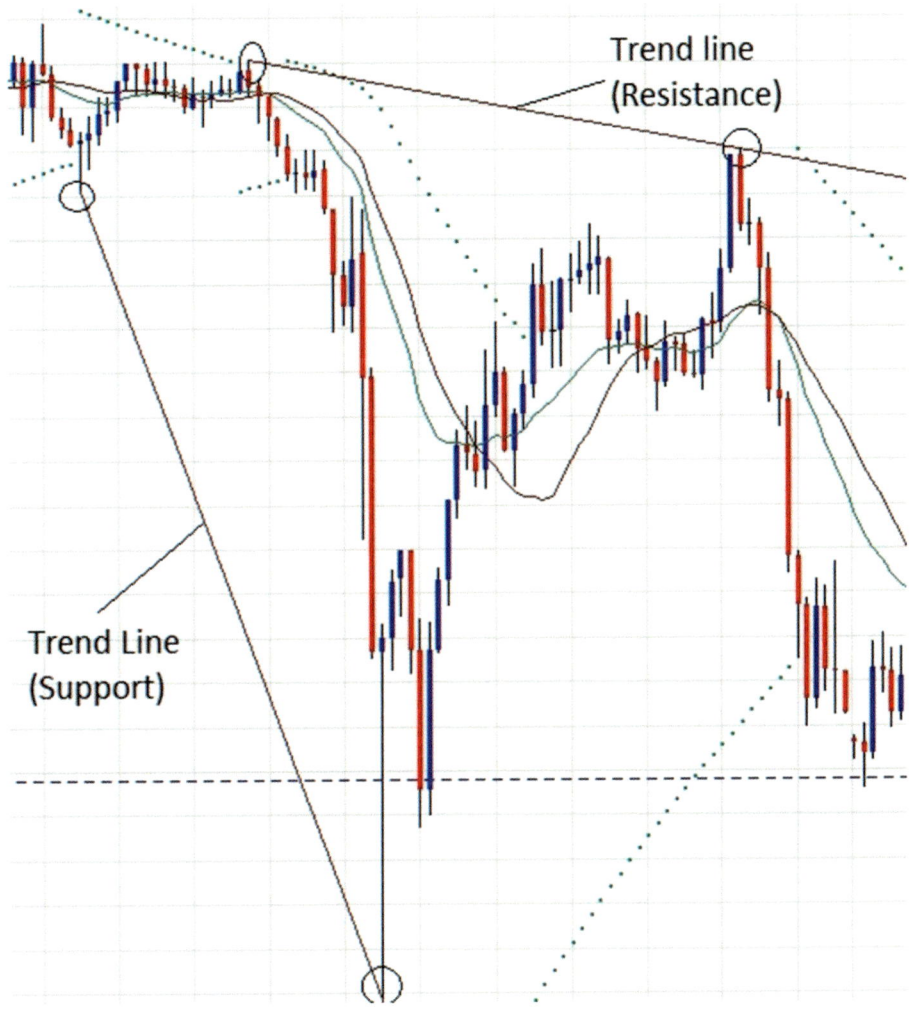

Chart 12: Current price is between trend lines

2. Fibonacci Retracements chart

After drawing trend lines, we draw Fibonacci retracements chart, the reason for this are:

- Fibonacci retracements lines are between trend lines (support and resistance), by having Fibonacci retracements line in between the trend lines we can locate the current price and EMA 20 whether they are inside the Fibonacci retracements lines or outside the lines.

- Before price moves from support to resistance or vice versa, the price movement need to pass Fibonacci retracement lines test before continuing its trend.

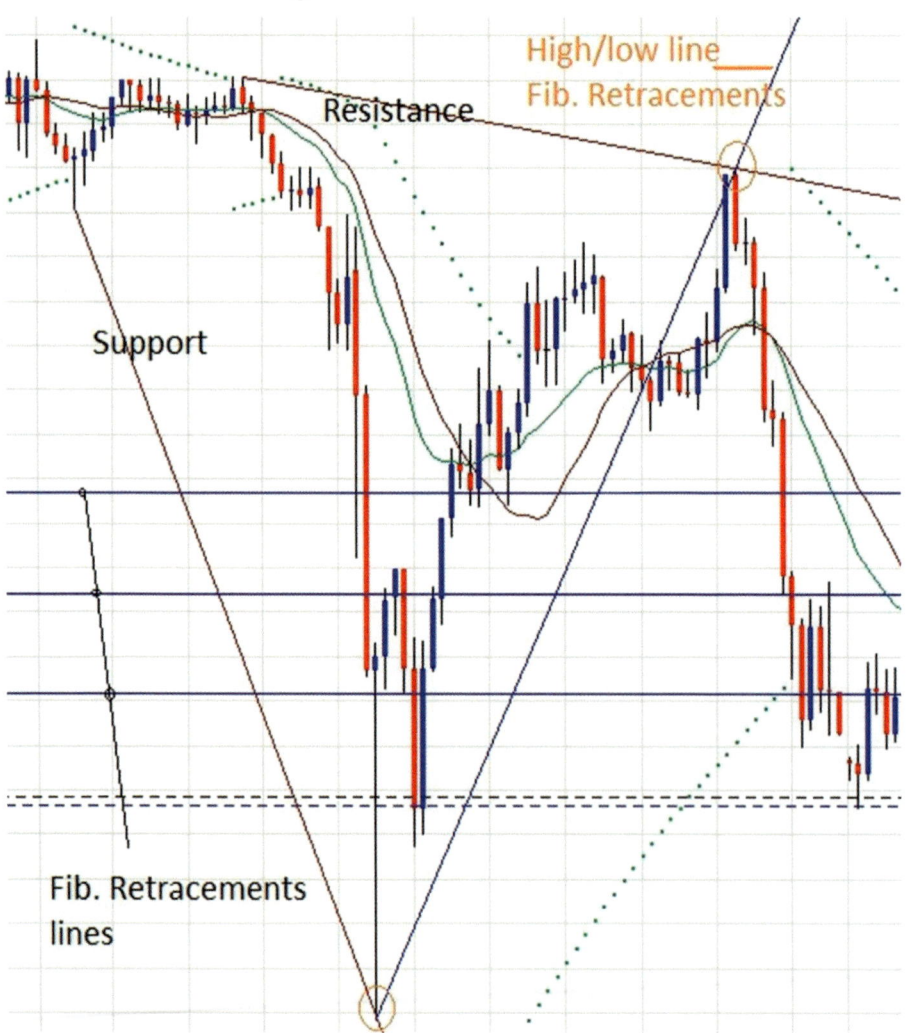

Chart 13: Fibonacci Retracements are between trend lines

3. Fibonacci Fan chart

Fibonacci Fan is preferred as step 3 than Fibonacci Extensions because Fibonacci Fan minor trend lines usually provide the nearest minor support and resistance (depend on the slope of trend lines) compared to Fibonacci extensions, however you can draw Fibonacci Fan and Extensions at the same time to find the nearest support and resistance

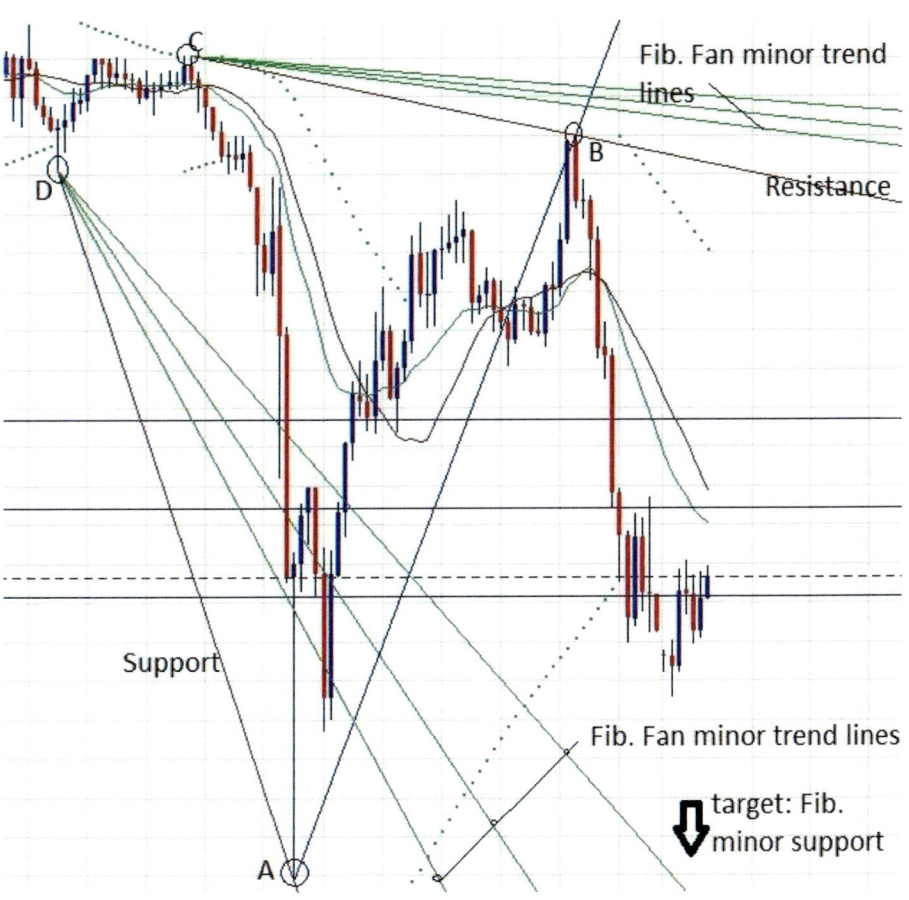

Chart 14: Fibonacci Retracements and Fan chart

4. Fibonacci Extensions chart

As explained before this Fibonacci Extensions chart can be presented at the same time with Fibonacci Fan and chart 15 is the final chart with Fibonacci Extension chart (pink color line both from support and resistance). After all Fibonacci charts are presented, we can notice that EMA 20 is still heading to the last/lowest Fibonaci Retracement line (X sign). Once EMA 20 breaks the lowest Fibonacci Retracement line, the next target price is Fibonacci Fan minor trend line (target on chart 15) and Fibonacci Extensions line (see target on chart 15) which ever line get hit first.

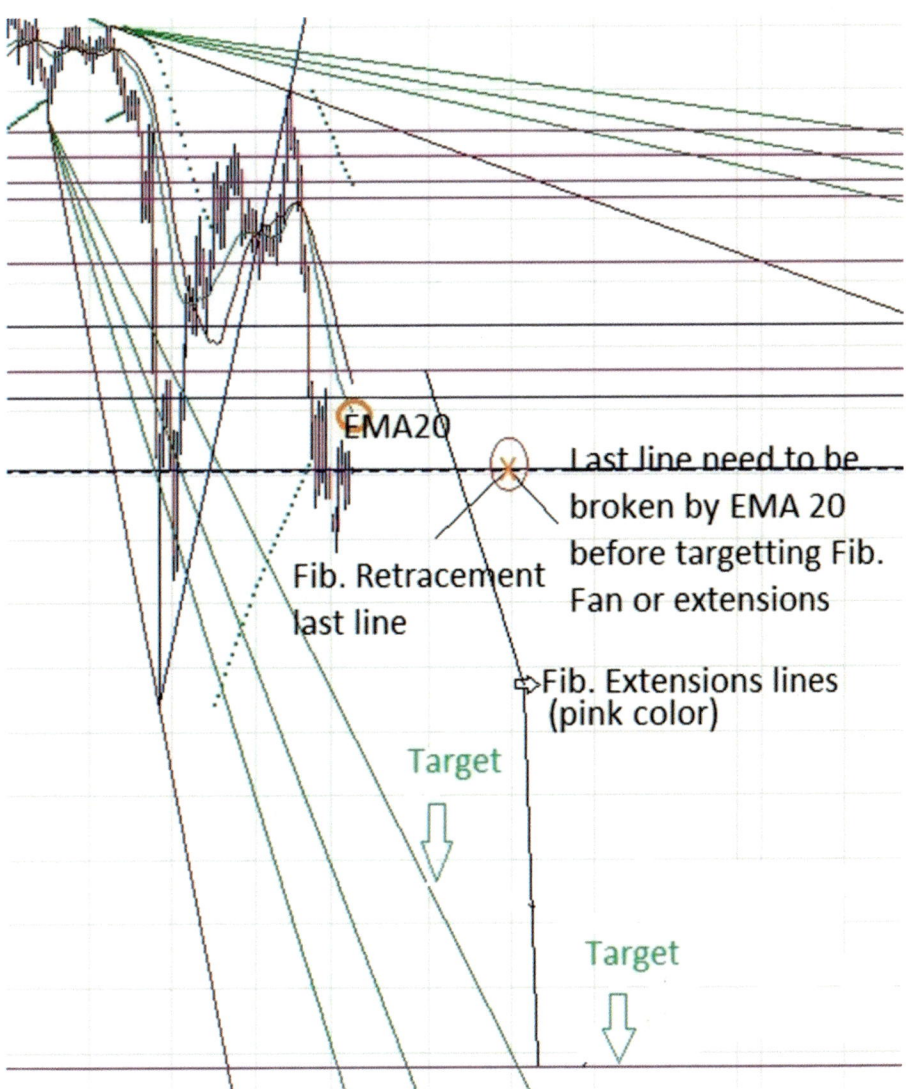

Chart 15: All Fibonacci charts

In chart 16 we can see that EMA 20 breaks the last line of Fib. Retracements lines and the next target is Fib. Fan lines or Fib. Extensions lines whichever get hit first

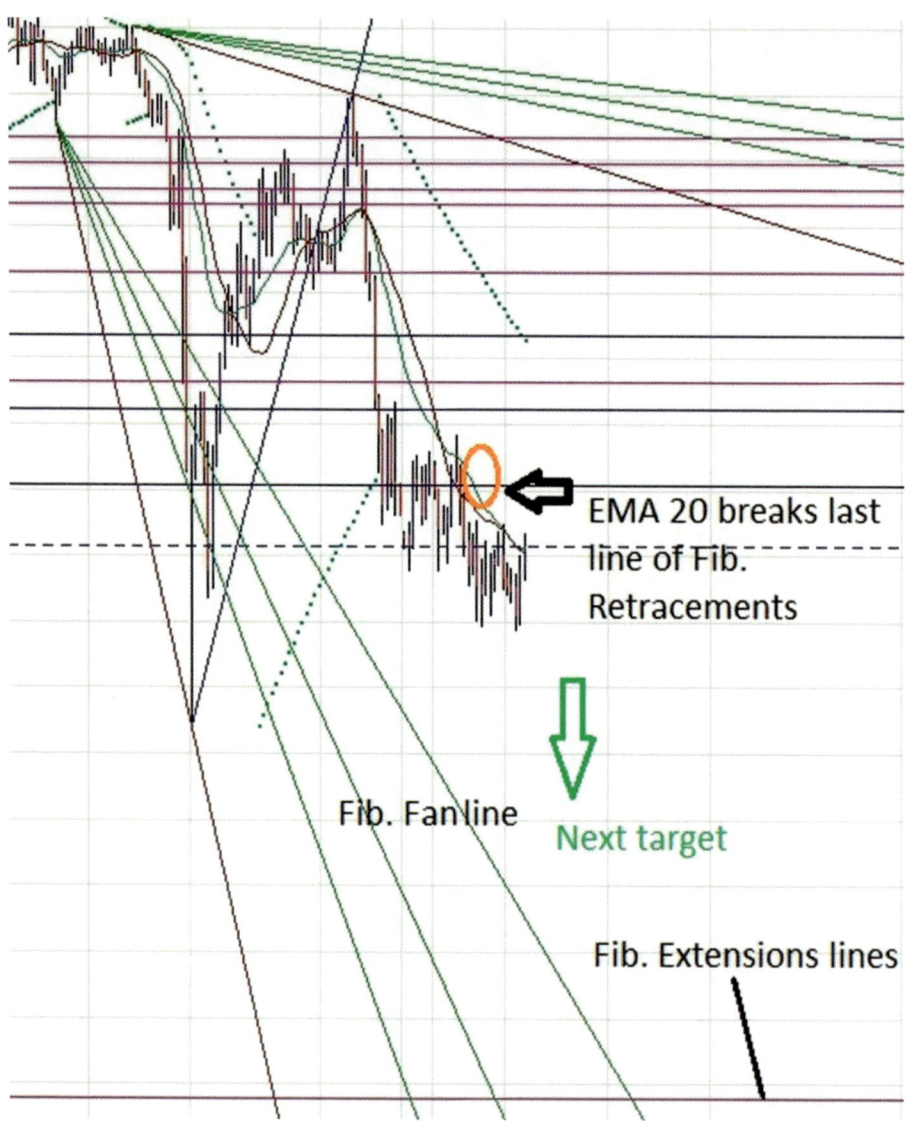

Chart 16: All Fibonacci charts- EMA 20 breaks Fib. Retracements line

CHAPTER 6

EXAMPLES

In this chapter you can observe some price movement and EMA 20 behaviors against trend lines and Fibonacci charts.

Example 1:

We are presenting an example by using currency market chart EUR/USD 1 hour chart dated 25th March 2015 (the analysis is also valid for other financial market i.e. commodities, futures, stocks, etc.)

Chart 17: Fibonacci Retracement

For better chart quality, we do not present the beginning point of support and resistance line and it is assume you know how to draw these basic trend lines; however we present RSI 14 for better explanation of the price movement.

Point A is the latest highest price within uptrend PSAR (0.02;0) group and point B is the lowest price within down trend PSAR (0.02;0) group.

Point C is where EMA 20 start entering the lowest Fibonacci Retracement line for its uptrend, although there is an attempt to reverse it by having price below EMA 20, the RSI 14 is still above 50 at point C

Point D is where EMA 20 start leaving the highest Fibonacci Retracement lines and there is a chance for uptrend continuation.

Point E is where the price below EMA 20 and SMA 20 and then RSI 14<50 which means potential reversal, however it fails to touch the highest Fibonacci Retracement line after several attempts.

At point F, the price is above EMA 20, SMA 20 and RSI>50 which means strong uptrend to move the price farther from the highest Fibonacci Retracements lines.

After we finish with the Fibonacci Retracement chart we want to know the next barriers by using Fibonacci Fan and Fibonacci Extensions charts, you can see chart 18 for all Fibonacci chart

Fibonacci Retracement lines are in blue color, Fibonacci Fan lines are in green color and Fibonacci Extensions lines are in pink colors.

Chart 18: All Fibonacci charts

Chart 18 is similar to chart 17; we just add Fibonacci Fan and Extension chart. Point F is where the price starts its uptrend however there are barrier at point G which are the Fibonacci Extension (pink lines) and Fibonacci Fan lines (green lines).

We can say that, when EMA 20 leaving Fibonacci retracement lines, there are several potential barriers from Fibonacci Fan and Extensions. As a rule of thumb: when the closing price cannot breaks the barrier twice, there is a chance for reversal especially when EMA 20 and SMA 20 cross plus RSI 14<50.

Example 2:

Chart 19: Trend lines and Fibonacci Retracement chart

Point B is the latest available highest price within uptrend PSAR (0.02;0) group and point D is the latest available lowest price within downtrend PSAR (0.02;0) group. By connecting point B and D we get Fibonacci Retracements lines

Chart 20 : Trend lines and Fibonacci Retracement chart analysis

After preparing Fibonacci Retracement lines by connecting point B and D, the price and EMA 20 is entering turbulence area E (Fib. Retracement lines). Once EMA 20 breaks the lowest Fib. Retracements lines at point F (see arrow), the price continue its downtrend, however there is an attempt to reverse the price and EMA 20 back to Fib. Retracement lines at point G however the price cannot touch the Fib. Retracements lines after several attempts at point H (rectangle)

Now let's see the complete Fibonacci charts after point H (rectangle) as presented in chart 21

.Chart 21: Trend lines and all Fibonacci chart analysis

Point I is where the price touch the nearest Fib. Fan (green line) and Fib. Extensions (pink line) line and bounce bank to point J after EMA 20 cross SMA 20 at point I.

After several attempt at point J, EMA 20 cannot breaks Fib. Extensions line (pink line) and it continues its down trend to nearest Fib. Extensions line and do some consolidations until EMA 20 breaks the Fib. Extensions line at point K and continue down trend to point L. It tries to reverse again at point M after EMA 20 cross SMA 20 and RSI>50.

CHAPTER 7

QUESTIONS AND ANSWERS

1. Why do we need to draw trend line when there are several barrier from Fibonacci chart, do we really need it?

Yes, we need to draw trend line first to provide support and resistance of price movement. The price moves faster than EMA 20 and the bold barrier is the trend line (resistance and support) so in each position it is better to take profit a few pips before trend line and see whether the price can breaks the trend line in two closing prices. Please also notice that there is turbulence in Fibonacci Retracements lines and take necessary action when there is a reversal sign (EMA 20 cross SMA20, and RSI 14) before the price hit the trend line. As long as the price keeps stable above EMA 20 for uptrend and below EMA 20 for down trend, there is a chance for trend continuation.

2. Should we update the Fibonacci chart for each PSAR reversal?

We need to update trend lines when there is PSAR reversal (around 3 support and 3 resistance lines), however for Fibonacci charts, you will get confused if you updated them in each PSAR reversal. You can keep current Fibonacci charts and update them with new Fibonacci charts after EMA 20 has left all the Fibonacci chart lines (Fib. Retracements, Fan and Extensions lines).

In summary: whenever you start, the last available PSAR (0.02;0) to draw trend lines and Fibonacci charts will become base charts for analysis and you update the Fibonacci charts when EMA 20 breaks all those Fibonacci lines.

3. Should we draw all Fibonacci charts at the same time?

It is better to draw trend lines and Fibonacci retracements chart first before adding other Fibonacci charts. Fibonacci retracements can give basic info on current price movement and EMA 20 position. If we finish analyzing Fibonacci Retracement chart, we continue with Fibonacci Fan and Extensions chart to see potential price target.

-   End   -

19290620R00022

Printed in Great Britain
by Amazon